The DUET BOOK

THE BEST OF CONTEMPORARY SONGS

ARRANGED BY TOM FETTKE

 **Lillenas** PUBLISHING COMPANY

KANSAS CITY, MO 64141

In All of His Glory

B. M. and D. D.

BABBIE MASON and DONNA DOUGLAS
Arr. by Tom Fettke

I Will Rejoice

M. W. S. and B. D.

MICHAEL W. SMITH and BEVERLY DARNALL
Arr. by Tom Fettke

I will_ re - joice_____ 'til the depths_ of my soul can sing.

19 **CD 1:07** *2nd time*

God reigns,___ let the earth pro - claim; Lift high___ His_ name

2nd time to Coda

'til the heav - ens shout back the same. I_____ will_____ re -

CD 1:06

joice, re - joice!

The Strength of the Lord

P. McH.

PHILL McHUGH
Arr. by Tom Fettke

When Praise Demands a Sacrifice

S. C. S. and R. M.

SUE C. SMITH and RUSSELL MAULDIN
Arr. by Tom Fettke

26

Another Time, Another Place

G. D.

GARY DRISKELL
Arr. by Bryce Inman
Edited by Tom Fettke

1. I've al-ways heard there is a land_____ be-yond the
(2.) tired of earth - ly things;_____ they prom - ise

*Voice 1, preferably male. Voice 2, preferably female

to an-oth-er time and an-oth - er place.

to an-oth-er time and an-oth - er place.

CD 1:18

2. I've___ grown so

er place.

er place.

CD 1:20

Lamb of God

T. P.

TWILA PARIS
Arr. by Tom Fettke

Peace in the Midst of the Storm

S. R. A.

STEPHEN R. ADAMS
Arr. by Russell Mauldin
Duet arr. by Tom Fettke

50

Seekers of Your Heart

M. T., D. T. and B. D.

MELODIE and DICK TUNNEY
and BEVERLY DARNALL
Arr. by Tom Fettke

*If this is too low for Voice 1, Voice 2 may sing until measure 12 on both verses.

How Great the Love

D. W.

DAN WHITTEMORE
Arr. by Joseph Linn
Duet arr. by Tom Fettke

No More Night

W. H.

WALT HARRAH
Arr. by Tom Fettke

With joyful anticipation ♩ = ca. 84

The time-less theme— earth and heav-en will pass a-way. It's not a dream, God will

Carry the Light

T. W.

TWILA PARIS
Arr. by Tom Fettke

Fervently ♩ = ca. 76

CD 1:40

1. In this world of dark - ness
2. Count them by the mil - lions,

we are giv - en____ light,
blind - ed slaves to____ sin.

Hope for all the
In - side, they are

Lion of Judah

R. B. and S. M.
Freely ♩ = ca. 76

RAY BOLTZ and STEVE MILLIKAN
Arr. by Tom Fettke

1. Mes - si - ah would come,_____ the earth would re - joice,_____ the peo - ple start____ to sing._____ For

2. No el - e - gant robes,_____ no glo - ri - ous throne,_____ no ar - mies at____ His side._____ Could

77

I Want to Know Christ

MICHAEL HUDSON
Flowing ♪ = ca. 88

GARY DRISKELL
Arr. by Tom Fettke

life is re - deemed. I know I have found what some
way of the cross; So I count what I gain, and for -

CD 2:03

Voice 2 *mp*

2. I

know, yes, I want to know

Christ! _____ And the

things that en - tan - gle me, I lay them_ down– all the trea-sures and tro-phies of

His Strength Is Perfect

S. C. C. and J. S.

STEVEN CURTIS CHAPMAN and JERRY SALLEY
Arr. by Tom Fettke

He'll car - ry us when we can't car - ry on.

Raised in His pow - er, the weak be - come strong.

2nd time to Coda

His strength is per - fect; His strength is per - fect.

D.S. al Coda

CD 2:08

decresc.

He Is the Amen

D. R.

DAVID RITTER
Arr. by D. R. and Tom Fettke

Embrace the Cross

J. E.

JOHN ELLIOTT
Arr. by Joseph Linn
Duet arr. by Tom Fettke

All the Glory Belongs to Jesus

GLORIA GAITHER

WILLIAM J. GAITHER
Arr. by Tom Fettke

Hallelujah! Praise the Lamb

P. T., D. T. and G. M.

PAM THUM, DAWN THOMAS
and GARY McSPADDEN
Arr. by Mosie Lister
Duet arr. by Tom Fettke

God and God Alone

P. McH.

PHILL McHUGH
Arr. by Tom Fettke

All Because of God's Amazing Grace

S. R. A.

STEPHEN R. ADAMS
Arr. by Mosie Lister
Duet arr. by Tom Fettke

cause on Cal-v'ry's moun-tain He took my place.

And some-day, some glo-rious morn-ing I shall

see Him face to face; And it's all be-cause of

CD 2:31

Voice 2

God's great grace. 2. Through

O Calvary's Lamb

C. B., B. G. and T. G.

CHARLES BOSARGE, BILL GEORGE and TOMMY GREER
Arr. by Marty Parks
Duet arr. by Tom Fettke

He Is Here

K. T.

KIRK TALLEY
Arr. by Tom Fettke

bless His name a - gain.___ He is here; lis - ten close - ly. Hear Him

bless His name a - gain.___ He is here; lis - ten close - ly. Hear Him

call - ing out___ your name. He is here; you___ can

call - ing out___ your name. He is here; you can

CD 2:39

touch Him. You will nev - er be the same.

touch Him. You will nev - er be___ the same.

23 *Voice 1*

I sense an awe - some mov-ing of the Ho - ly Spir - it.

27 *Voice 2*

I see His coun - te - nance rest - ing on your face.

31 *Voices 1 and 2*
Unison   *Div.* mel.

I know that there are an - gels hov-'ring all a-round us,___ For the

35

CD 2:40
cresc.   *mf*

pres - ence of the Lord is in this place.   He is

cresc.

Daystar
(Shine Down on Me)

S. R.

STEVE RICHARDSON
Arr. by Joseph Linn
Duet arr. by Tom Fettke

With feeling ♩ = ca. 69

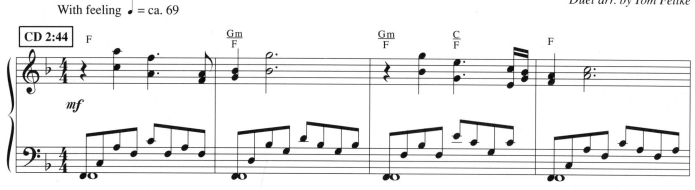

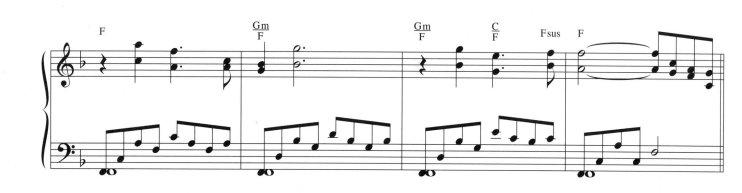

8   *1st verse: Voice 1*
    2nd verse: Voice 2

1. Li - ly of the Val - ley, let Your sweet a - ro - ma fill my
   see a world that's dy - ing, wound - ed by the mas - ter of de -

He Loved Me

D. H.

DOUG HOLCK and TOM FETTKE
Arr. by Tom Fettke

Narration: God chose us to be His very own before the creation of the world. "He decided then to make us holy in His eyes, without a single fault—we who stand before Him covered with His love.

His unchanging plan has always been to adopt us into His own family by sending Jesus Christ to die for us. And He did this because He wanted to!" *(Eph. 1:4-5, TLB)* *

*From *The Living Bible*, © 1971 by Tyndale House Publishers, Wheaton, IL.

142